From Len & Henriette
Christmas 1977

Proverbs to Live By

editor and publisher
Maryjane Hooper Tonn

A proverb is a short sentence based on long experience.

Miguel de Cervantes

Managing Editor, Ralph Luedtke
Associate Editor, Julie Hogan
Photographic Editor, Gerald Koser
Production Editor, Stuart L. Zyduck

IDEALS PUBLISHING CORP., MILWAUKEE, WIS. 53201
© COPYRIGHT MCMLXXVII, PRINTED AND BOUND IN U.S.A.
ISBN 0-89542-144-5 375

CONTENTS

AGE

Age does not depend upon years, but upon temperament and health. Some men are born old and some never grow old. *(Edwards)*

❧☙

Age is opportunity, not less than youth itself, though in another dress. *(Longfellow)*

❧☙

The old age of an eagle is better than the youth of a sparrow. *(Greek)*

❧☙

It is less painful to learn in youth than to be ignorant in age.

❧☙

Young people must be taught, old ones honored. *(Danish)*

No one is so old as to think he cannot live one more year. *(Cicero)*

One is as old as one's heart. *(d'Houdetot)*

No wise man ever wished to be younger. *(Swift)*

We do not count a man's years until
he has nothing else to count. *(Emerson)*

Age should not have its face lifted but rather teach the world to
admire wrinkles as the etchings of experience and the firm lines
of character. *(Perry)*

AMBITION

To the man who himself strives earnestly, God also lends a helping hand. *(Aeschylus)*

To him who is determined it remains only to act. *(Italian)*

God helps them who help themselves. *(Franklin)*

Would you rise in the world, veil ambition with the forms of humanity. *(Chinese)*

The journey of a thousand miles starts with a single step. *(Chinese)*

No one knows what he can do till he tries. *(Latin)*

❦

A great deal of talent is lost in this world for want of a little courage. *(Smith)*

❦

There is no eel so small but it hopes to become a whale. *(German)*

❦

The greatest thing in the world is not so much where we stand as in what direction we are moving. *(Holmes)*

❦

So high as a tree aspires to grow, so high will it find an atmosphere suited to it. *(Thoreau)*

❦

If you want a thing done, do it yourself. *(Rousseau)*

ART

Art is the path of the creator to his work. *(Emerson)*

Art never expresses anything but itself. *(Wilde)*

Art strives for form, and hopes for beauty. *(Bellows)*

As the sun colors flowers so does art color life. *(Lubbock)*

Great art is an instant arrested in eternity. *(Hunekar)*

Let each man exercise the art he knows. *(Aristophanes)*

Art is not a thing: it is a way. *(Elbert Hubbard)*

All great art is the expression of man's delight
in God's work—not his own. *(Ruskin)*

Art is a shadow of Divine perfection. *(Michelangelo)*

All art is but imitation of nature. *(Seneca)*

BEAUTY

The beauty seen is partly in him who sees it. *(Bovee)*

A thing of beauty is a joy forever. *(Keats)*

What is beautiful is good, and who
is good will soon also be beautiful.
(Sappho)

Beauty is the gift of God. *(Aristotle)*

Beauty seen is never lost. *(Whittier)*

Everything has its beauty but not everyone sees it. *(Confucius)*

CHARACTER

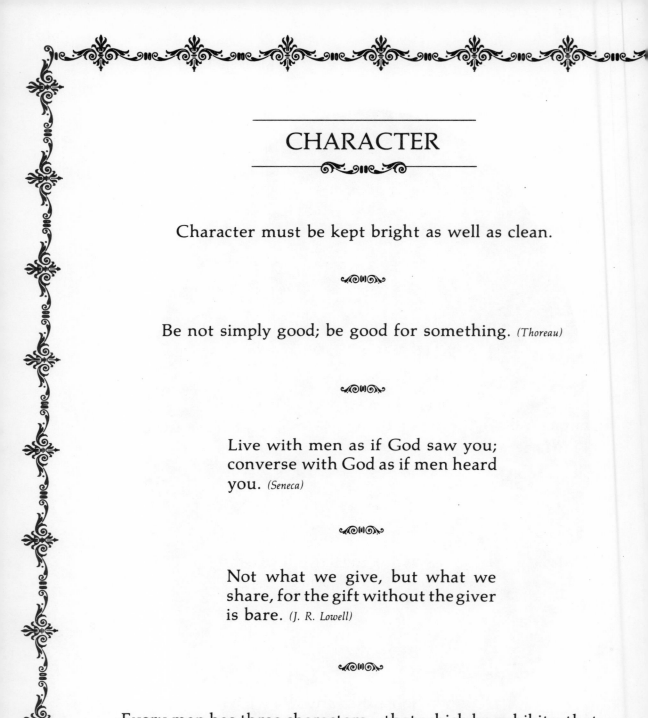

Character must be kept bright as well as clean.

Be not simply good; be good for something. *(Thoreau)*

Live with men as if God saw you; converse with God as if men heard you. *(Seneca)*

Not what we give, but what we share, for the gift without the giver is bare. *(J. R. Lowell)*

Every man has three characters—that which he exhibits, that which he has, and that which he thinks he has. *(Karr)*

It matters not what you are
thought to be, but what you are.
(Latin)

Character is habit long continued. *(Greek)*

Character is the result of two things—mental attitude and the
way we spend our time. *(Hubbard)*

If you wish your merit to be known,
acknowledge that of other people.
(Oriental)

Do not choose for anyone what
you do not choose for yourself.
(Persian)

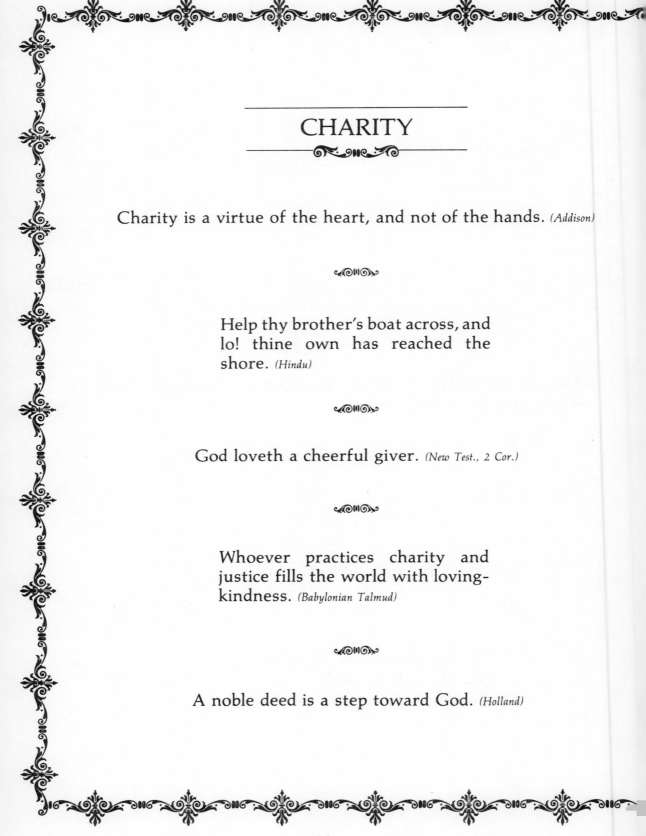

CHARITY

Charity is a virtue of the heart, and not of the hands. *(Addison)*

Help thy brother's boat across, and lo! thine own has reached the shore. *(Hindu)*

God loveth a cheerful giver. *(New Test., 2 Cor.)*

Whoever practices charity and justice fills the world with loving-kindness. *(Babylonian Talmud)*

A noble deed is a step toward God. *(Holland)*

Above all things have fervent charity among yourselves. *(New Test., Peter)*

⁂

Charity begins at home. *(Latin)*

⁂

Without dew and light flowers fade. Charity and love are the dew and light of the human heart. *(De Gentis)*

⁂

He is truly great who hath a great charity. *(Thomas a Kempis)*

⁂

The hand that gives, gathers. *(Ray)*

⁂

The most acceptable service of God is doing good to man. *(Franklin)*

CHILDREN

When a child stumbles, a good angel puts his hands under. *(Yiddish)*

Follow a child and you will find yourself at the very gateway of love, joy, and sincerity. *(Underhill)*

Let thy child's first lesson be obedience.

Children are the keys of Paradise. *(Stoddard)*

It is better to bind children by respect than by fear. *(Latin)*

Happy is he that is happy in his children.

⁂

The childhood shows the man, as morning shows the day. *(Milton)*

⁂

Where children are not, heaven is not.

⁂

A child is not a vessel to be filled, but a lamp to be lighted.

⁂

Children have more need of models than of critics. *(French)*

⁂

A child is a guest in the house, to be loved and respected, never possessed, for he is a gift of God. *(Salinger)*

CONFIDENCE

Confidence is the companion of success.

❧⦿❧

He who wills, can.

❧⦿❧

They can because they think they can. *(Vergil)*

❧⦿❧

Ability without confidence and determination is of no practical value to anyone. *(Vanbee)*

❧⦿❧

Be sure you're right, then go ahead. *(Crockett)*

❧⦿❧

Confidence placed in another often compels confidence in return. *(Latin)*

DIFFICULTY

All things are difficult before they are easy.

Nothing is difficult to a willing mind.

It is difficulties which show what men are. *(Greek)*

The best things are most difficult. *(Greek)*

The greater the difficulty, the greater the glory. *(Latin)*

Any job done reluctantly is a difficult one. *(Vanbee)*

ERROR

Who errs and mends, to God himself commends. *(Shelton)*

The shortest errors are always the best. *(Charron)*

Even the wisest of the wise may err. *(Aeschylus)*

To err and learn, is far better than never to err at all.

Do not condemn the judgment of another because it differs from your own, as you may both be in error. *(Dandemis)*

Fool me once, shame on you; fool me twice, shame on me. *(Chinese)*

EXPERIENCE

Experience is the father of wisdom, and memory the mother.

Q

In almost everything, experience is
more valuable than precept. *(Quintilian)*

Q

Experience is not what happens to a man. It is what a man does
with what happens to him. *(Huxley)*

Q

One thorn of experience is worth a
whole wilderness of warning. *(Lowell)*

You shall know by experience. *(Latin)*

It is costly wisdom that is bought by experience.

Experience joined with common sense, to mortals is a providence.
(Green)

He knows the water best who has waded through it. *(Danish)*

Experience is forever sowing the seed of one thing after another.
(Manilius)

FAITH

Belief is a truth held in the mind, faith is a fire in the heart. *(Newton)*

Faith is the force of life. *(Tolstoy)*

Faith is a certitude without proofs. *(French)*

The future always holds something for the man who keeps his faith in it.

All things proclaim the existence of God. *(Napoleon)*

The faith to move mountains is the reward of those who have moved little hills.

The flower that follows the sun does so even on cloudy days. *(Leighton)*

A perfect faith lifts us above fear.

Faith is love taking the form of aspiration. *(Channing)*

All that we have seen should teach us
to trust the Creator for what we have not seen.

What is faith unless it is to believe
what you do not see. *(St. Augustine)*

Faith goes up the stairs that love has made and looks out of the windows which hope has opened. *(Spurgeon)*

Faith in tomorrow makes today beautiful. *(Mobley)*

Faith is not a sense, nor sight, nor reason,
but taking God at his word. *(Evans)*

Faith is the pencil of the soul
that pictures heavenly things. *(Burbridge)*

Faith is the substance of things hoped for, the evidence of
things not seen. *(New Test., Heb.)*

Faith is to believe what we do not see; and the reward of this
faith is to see what we believe. *(St. Augustine)*

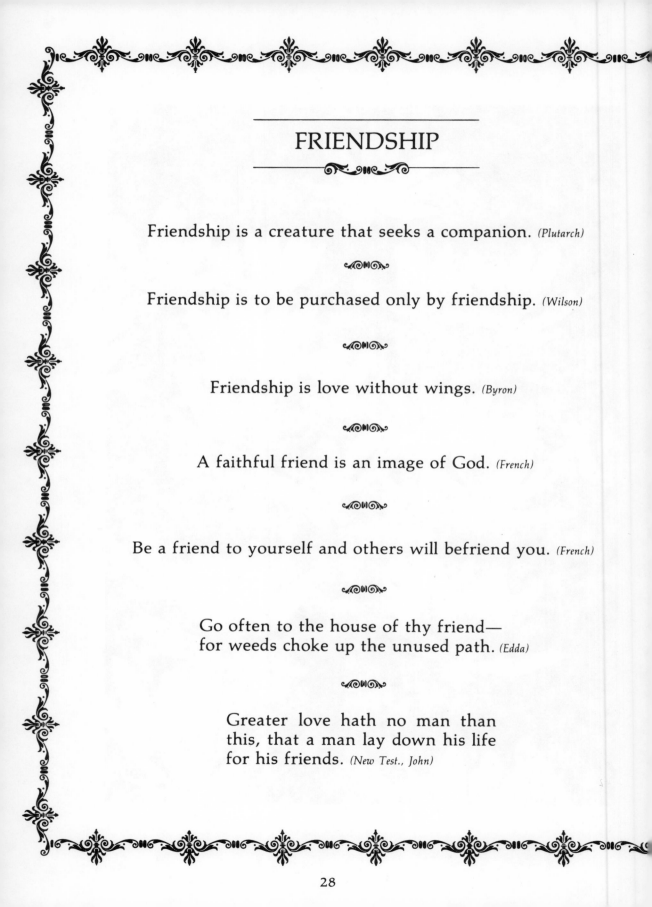

FRIENDSHIP

Friendship is a creature that seeks a companion. *(Plutarch)*

Friendship is to be purchased only by friendship. *(Wilson)*

Friendship is love without wings. *(Byron)*

A faithful friend is an image of God. *(French)*

Be a friend to yourself and others will befriend you. *(French)*

Go often to the house of thy friend—
for weeds choke up the unused path. *(Edda)*

Greater love hath no man than
this, that a man lay down his life
for his friends. *(New Test., John)*

A faithful friend is the medicine of life. *(Apocrypha)*

❧⊙❦⊚☙

A friend in need is a friend indeed.

❧⊙❦⊚☙

A friend is a person with whom I may be sincere. *(Emerson)*

❧⊙❦⊚☙

Do good by thy friend to keep him,
to thy enemy to gain him. *(Franklin)*

❧⊙❦⊚☙

The only way to have a friend is to be one.

❧⊙❦⊚☙

They are rich who have true friends.

❧⊙❦⊚☙

Actions, not words, are the true characteristic mark of the
attachment of friends. *(Washington)*

HAPPINESS

The chiefest point of happiness is that a man should be willing to be what he is. *(Erasmus)*

Man is the artificer of his own happiness. *(Thoreau)*

He that thinks himself the happiest man, really is so. *(Colton)*

It is neither wealth, nor splendor, but tranquillity and occupation, which give happiness. *(Jefferson)*

A happy life consists in tranquillity of mind. *(Cicero)*

Life is a mirror: if you frown at it, it frowns back; if you smile, it returns the greeting. *(Thackeray)*

Always turn your face to the sun,
and the shadows will fall behind you.

The city of happiness is in the country of expectancy and the state of mind.

Following happiness is like chasing
the wind, or clutching the shadow.
(Japanese)

Be glad of life because it gives you the chance to love and to work and to play and to look at the stars. *(van Dyke)*

Give to the world the best you have
and the best will come back to you.

The way to be happy is to make others so. *(Ingersoll)*

HONESTY

Too much honesty did never man harm.

Honesty is the best policy.

It is man that makes truth great,
not truth that makes man great.
(Confucius)

Honest men fear neither the light nor the dark.

He that loseth his honesty hath nothing else to lose. *(Lyly)*

You may measure every man's honesty by your own.

HOPE

Hope is the thing with feathers that perches in the soul. *(Dickinson)*

The greatest architect and the one most needed is hope. *(Beecher)*

Hope is the dream of a waking man. *(Diogenes)*

It is hope which maintains most of mankind. *(Sophocles)*

Everything that is done in the world is done by hope. *(Luther)*

Hope springs eternal in the human breast. *(Pope)*

Hope is the parent of faith.

As long as there is life there is hope.

Great hopes make great men.

Hope is like the sun which, as we journey towards it, casts the shadow of our burden behind it. *(Smiles)*

HUMILITY

All prayer needeth humiliation. *(Apocrypha)*

He that is humble, ever shall have God to be his guide. *(Bunyan)*

Nearest the throne itself must be the footstool of humility. *(Montgomery)*

There is no true holiness without humility.

The higher we are placed, the more humbly should we walk. *(Cicero)*

Humble thyself in all things. *(Thomas a Kempis)*

Rather to bow than break is profit-
able; humility is a thing commend-
able. *(French)*

By humility and the fear of the Lord are riches, and honour,
and life. *(Old Test., Prov.)*

If thou desire greatness, be humble;
no other ladder is there by which to
climb. *(Sadi)*

Humility is to make a right estimate of one's self. *(Spurgeon)*

The crown of a good disposition is humility. *(Burckhardt)*

HUMOR

He is not laughed at that laughs at himself first.

Laugh, and the world laughs with
you, weep, and you weep alone.
(E. W. Wilcox)

The laughter of man is the contentment of God.

He deserves Paradise who makes
his companions laugh. *(Mohammed)*

A good laugh is sunshine in the house.

A face without a smile is like a lantern without a light. *(Reeves)*

KNOWLEDGE

As a field, however fertile, cannot be fruitful without cultivation, neither can a mind without learning. *(Cicero)*

A man is but what he knoweth. *(Bacon)*

An investment in knowledge pays the best interest. *(Franklin)*

It is better to know something about everything than all about one thing. *(Pascal)*

To know one's ignorance is the best part of knowledge. *(Chinese)*

Knowledge is the wing wherewith we fly to heaven. *(Shakespeare)*

Knowledge is the action of the soul.

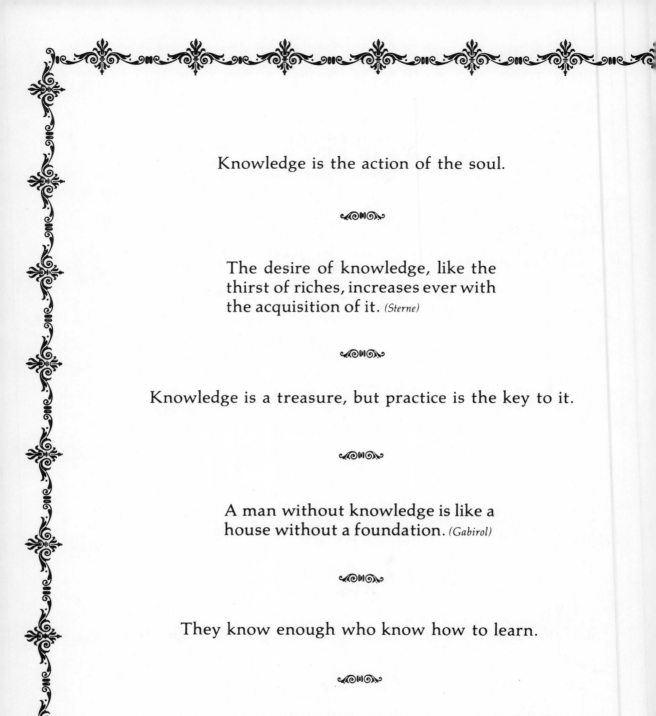

The desire of knowledge, like the thirst of riches, increases ever with the acquisition of it. *(Sterne)*

Knowledge is a treasure, but practice is the key to it.

A man without knowledge is like a house without a foundation. *(Gabirol)*

They know enough who know how to learn.

If you have knowledge, let others light their candles at it. *(Fuller)*

LABOR

Every man's work is always a portrait of himself. *(Butler)*

Blessed is he who has found his work; let him ask no other blessedness. *(Carlyle)*

The best preparation for tomorrow's work is to do your work as well as you can today. *(Hubbard)*

In all labor there is profit. *(Old Test., Prov.)*

He that hath a trade hath an estate. *(Franklin)*

He that labors and thrives spins gold.

⟡

Honest labor bears a lovely face.

⟡

To him that toils God owes glory. *(Greek)*

⟡

To labor is to pray. *(Latin)*

⟡

He who would eat the kernel must crack the shell. *(Latin)*

Honor lies in honest toil.

By the work one knows the workman. *(La Fontaine)*

When you have set yourself a task, finish it. *(Ovid)*

Properly speaking, all true work is religion. *(Carlyle)*

The work of life alone teaches us to value the good of life. *(Goethe)*

LOVE

Love is love's reward.

Sometimes love has been implanted by a single glance. *(Burckhardt)*

Love is the blossom where there blows everything that lives or grows.

Love needs no teaching.

A flower cannot live without sunshine and man cannot live without love. *(Muller)*

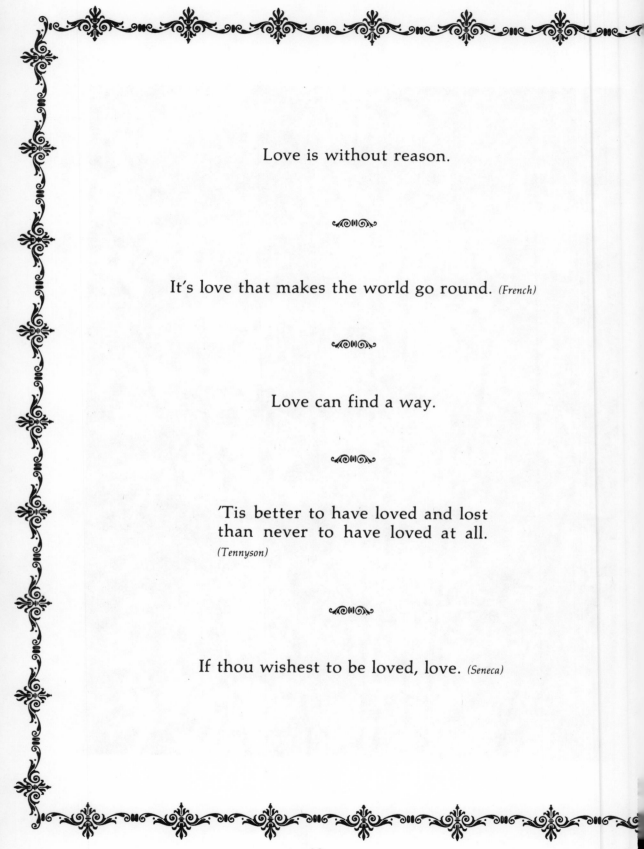

Love is without reason.

It's love that makes the world go round. *(French)*

Love can find a way.

'Tis better to have loved and lost than never to have loved at all. *(Tennyson)*

If thou wishest to be loved, love. *(Seneca)*

They do not love that do not show their love.

≈⊙⋈⊙≈

Love is stronger than death. *(French)*

≈⊙⋈⊙≈

Love begets love. *(Latin)*

≈⊙⋈⊙≈

When we love, it is the heart that judges. *(French)*

≈⊙⋈⊙≈

A book upon love is almost always an autobiography. *(Simon)*

MEMORY

The true art of memory is the art of attention. *(Johnson)*

Memory is the treasury of all things and their guardian. *(Cicero)*

Attention is the stuff that memory is made of,
and memory is accumulated genius. *(Lowell)*

Memory, of all the powers of the
mind, is the most delicate and frail.
(Jonson)

A good memory is one that is so poor that you can't remember
what you worried about yesterday.

A good memory is often as ready a friend as a sharp wit. *(Fuller)*

MUSIC

Music is love in search of a word. *(Lanier)*

Song brings of itself a cheerfulness
that wakes the heart of joy. *(Euripides)*

Music is well said to be the speech of angels. *(Carlyle)*

Instruments sound sweetest when
they be touched softest. *(Lyly)*

The man who has music in his soul
will be most in love with the
loveliest. *(Plato)*

Music is the medicine of a troubled mind. *(Latin)*

Music hath charms to soothe the savage breast. *(Congreve)*

Music is the speech of angels. *(Carlyle)*

Music is the eye of the ear.

Music—the only universal tongue.

Where words fail, music speaks. *(Anderson)*

NATURE

Nature is a volume of which God is the author.

To a rational being, to act according
to nature and according to reason
is the same thing. *(Aurelius)*

Nature will have its course.

Nature, to be commanded, must be obeyed. *(Bacon)*

Live according to nature. *(Latin)*

One touch of nature makes the whole world kin. *(Shakespeare)*

Nature does nothing in vain. *(Latin)*

The wisest, happiest of our kind are they
That ever walk content with Nature's way. *(Wordsworth)*

Nature is the art of God. *(Dante)*

Nothing is great but the inexhaustible wealth of nature. *(Emerson)*

OPPORTUNITY

As we have therefore opportunity,
let us do good unto all men. *(New Test., Gal.)*

A wise man will make more opportunities than he finds. *(Bacon)*

Never leave till tomorrow that which you can do today. *(Franklin)*

While we consider when to begin, it becomes too late. *(Latin)*

A man would do nothing, if he waited until he could do it so well that no one would find fault with what he has done. *(Cardinal Newman)*

If Heaven drops a date, open your mouth. *(Champion)*

An occasion lost cannot be redeemed.

He who seizes the right moment is the right man. *(Goethe)*

Strike while the iron is hot.

He who will not when he may, may not when he will. *(Latin)*

A man must make his opportunity as oft as find it. *(Bacon)*

A year's opportunities depend on the spring, a day's on the dawn, a family's on harmony, a life's on industry. *(Confucius)*

No great man ever complains of want of opportunity. *(Emerson)*

PATIENCE

He that can have patience can have what he will.

Patience opens all doors.

Let patience grow in your garden.

Patience is the best medicine there is for a sick man.

Patience is a virtue. *(Chaucer)*

The world is for him who has patience. *(Italian)*

Patience reaps peace, and rashness regret; the former riches, the latter poverty. *(Gabirol)*

Our patience will achieve more than our force. *(Burke)*

Patience is the key to Paradise. *(Turkish)*

An ounce of patience is worth a pound of brains. *(Dutch)*

TIME

All the treasures of earth cannot
bring back one lost moment. *(French)*

Even as we speak, envious Time has fled. *(Horace)*

A stitch in time saves nine.

Time, like an everflowing stream,
bears all things onwards. *(Plutarch)*

Gather ye rosebuds while ye may,
Old Time is still a-flying. *(Herrick)*

Time heals sorrow.

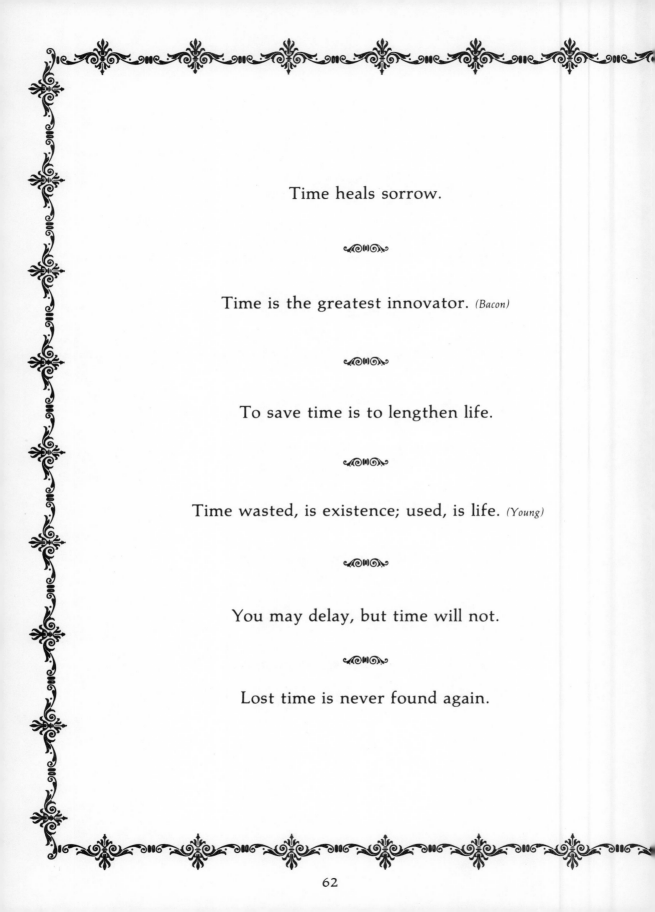

Time is the greatest innovator. *(Bacon)*

To save time is to lengthen life.

Time wasted, is existence; used, is life. *(Young)*

You may delay, but time will not.

Lost time is never found again.

As time hurts, so does time cure.

❦

Time measures nothing but itself. *(Thoreau)*

❦

Waste neither time nor money, but
make the best use of both. *(Franklin)*

❦

Time is God's, not ours. *(Dutch)*

❦

There is a time for all things. *(Old. Test., Eccles.)*

❦

An inch of time cannot be bought by an inch of gold. *(Chinese)*

WISDOM

Men would be wise, if they did not think themselves wise. *(Gracián)*

Early to bed and early to rise, makes a man healthy, wealthy and wise. *(Franklin)*

He is a wise man who does not grieve for the things which he has not, but rejoices for those which he has. *(Epictetus)*

Some are wise, and some are otherwise. *(Howell)*